T0129677

GOD
SPEAKS
in
SILENCE

POEMS
for All
Seasons

WILFRED G. CHEN M.D.

WESTBOW
P R E S S®
A DIVISION OF THOMAS NELSON
& ZONDERVAN

Copyright © 2017 WILFRED G. CHEN M.D.
B.Ch., B.A.O., M.B. HONS. N.U.I
Urology Research,
Carlton Centre,
San Fernando,
Trinidad and Tobago.
Tel: 868-652-4761 Mobile: 868-356-0018.
Email: wilfredgchen@hotmail.com

All rights reserved. No part of this book may be used or reproduced by
any means, graphic, electronic, or mechanical, including photocopying,
recording, taping or by any information storage retrieval system
without the written permission of the author except in the case of
brief quotations embodied in critical articles and reviews.

WestBow Press books may be ordered through booksellers or by contacting:

WestBow Press
A Division of Thomas Nelson & Zondervan
1663 Liberty Drive
Bloomington, IN 47403
www.westbowpress.com
1 (866) 928-1240

Because of the dynamic nature of the Internet, any web addresses or
links contained in this book may have changed since publication and
may no longer be valid. The views expressed in this work are solely those
of the author and do not necessarily reflect the views of the publisher,
and the publisher hereby disclaims any responsibility for them.

Any people depicted in stock imagery provided by Thinkstock are models,
and such images are being used for illustrative purposes only.
Certain stock imagery © Thinkstock.

ISBN: 978-1-9736-0327-6 (sc)
ISBN: 978-1-9736-0338-2 (hc)
ISBN: 978-1-9736-0328-3 (e)

Library of Congress Control Number: 2017915109

Print information available on the last page.

WestBow Press rev. date: 04/24/2018

IN GRATITUDE

IN GRATITUDE
To the LORD
through St. Josemaria Escriva,
Founder of Opus Dei,
who has inspired
and is inspiring millions,
seeking Holiness
in the world,
to be loved
with a passion
for Work and Family,
Contemplating God,
moment by moment,
Seeking a Perfection
of Silence and Stillness,
These times of Rush
And Madness.

THE PROFESSOR SPEAKS

The most striking aspect of this collection of poems by WILFRED G. CHEN is a deep sense of conviction in the goodness of God who created and now administers the world with merciful and loving care. This divinely ordered universe, in which people are made in the image of God, is strictly controlled, and either asserted or implied by the persona or speaking voice in almost every poem in the volume. In "Data Digestion," for instance, we are told: "Everyone is Imaged in the Likeness/ of the Creator/ Genius Almighty," while in "Contemplating in Silence," we are counselled that God is: "The Eternal Presence,/ the Eternal Silence,/ of Infinite Love/ of Mercy/ and of Power."

Some poems may invoke sympathy and compassion for victims of illness or misfortune, while others warn against temptations such as: "Calves of Gold, Concrete towers gleaming…/ Night life pleasures" as in "Racing Through Life;" but, as in "Time to go," repentance and forgiveness of sin are always available, and the door is never completely closed: "To a Home in the Distance/ A Home of Peace/ And Rest."

Yet, if the mainly abstract diction and a slightly hectoring tone in some poems arouse suspicions of forced or false piety, hinting at wishful thinking, other poems like "April Rain" win great conviction and achieve solid artistic success when they employ wholly credible, natural imagery to show how God's "Grace/ from Heaven filters/ slowly into our Souls/ like Raindrops falling/ from the sky." Similarly convincing, natural imagery is again seen in "In Retreat" where the persona rejoices in: "Wind whistling through Leaves/ Kiskidees Kingly Perched…in Silence/ like Trappist Monks/ in Hooded File."

Thus, through poems of simple diction and short lines, often consisting of no more than two or three words, Chen successfully communicates the sincerity and purity of his deeply-rooted, Catholic faith, and the transcendent genuineness of his religious vocation.

PROF. FRANK BIRBALSINGH
Professor Emeritus
York University, Canada.
Author of many books,
Judge for Commonwealth Literary Prize.

IN MEMORY

In memory of my parents John and Iris Chen
and grand mother Apo, immigrants from
Tientsin View, Kwong Tung Province, China,
who by Heavenly Design were brought thousands
of miles from their homeland village, planted in
this blessed land of the Trinity Trinidad and Tobago
baptized, late into their adult lives, bringing for
the first time, in their words, such inexpressible
Joy.

INTRODUCTION

It is a great joy to write this introduction to a small but precious collection of poems for a close friend of mine. Besides being a Physician for decades who experienced at first hand human suffering so mysterious in its myriad forms, Dr. Wilfred G. Chen M.D. is also a deeply spiritual person rooted in the Catholic Faith and its traditions. It is no surprise that this collection of poems 'gems of wisdom' centered on the Divine and suffused with human insights, is undoubtedly a product of an elevated spirituality cultivated in deep prayer, study and meditation over decades.

In this era of the global village, where mankind is becoming more robotic and addictive to modern technology, this booklet shall assist the contemporary person to be more human and focus on the Divine to attain inner peace and bliss. These poems are a veritable source in finding inner tranquility and equilibrium. May those who constantly meditate on them find that stability and inner enrichment, which the famous giant 4th century theologian of the Church St. Augustine transmitted to us "our hearts are restless until they rest in thee, O God."

These glittering poetic gems are also in keeping with a fine tradition of the Catholic Church – the motto of the Dominican Order (O.P.) "Contemplata aliis tradere," to hand over to others fruits of contemplation.

Dr. Wilfred G. Chen has given us a precious pocket book

to 21st century person for holistic healing and spiritual riches, anticipating the immeasurable eternal bliss to come.

Fr. Thomas Harricharan M.A.
Author and Researcher on
Church History of the Americas
and World Religions.

PREFACE

Written in simple lines, these poems convey the authority of a seasoned poet, whose sonorous and sentimental aspirations keep the readers involved in the context of their indepth meaning. Their smooth cadence is without the cacophonous grittiness that dispels the imagination and fellowship of the reader's mind to positive pursuit of peace and happiness. All thoughts, references and ideas qualifying the religious appurtenances are strong with an appeal to a wide range of people of all form of worship. And it is this universal theme that attracts, as it deals with a Divine relevance to the truth and strength of an interior life.

These poems beckon attention and compel enthusiasm by their appeal to the heavenly domain and the Master of Life, and here is the evidence of the manifold enrichment of the ideal theme, that is the governing factor of urgency. This quality alone make these poems outstanding, putting them in a class of their own.

In their simplicity of the eclectic variables of tonal appeal, this collection is accredited with a sameness of a common viewpoint. Yet each poem is enshrined with a particular justification of thoughtful intelligence, and makes the reading appeal to everyone irrespective of race, religion, sex or age, area of location or political affiliation.

WILLI CHEN H.B.M., C.M.T.
Sculptor, Dramatist, Painter, Writer, Shortlisted for the Commonwealth Literary Prize.

FOREWORD

In this very handy portable collection of poems you will find God's plenty. The poems are unpretentious creations that are deceptively simple, yet very accessible to people from all walks of life. Herein lies its power and appeal as the poet draws his audience into the construct of his poems moving them to grasp the essential of his themes. The poems are easy to enter, and enables one to grasp what poetry is about: essentially, a lyric slowing of time to pay proper reverent attention to the given world.

Chen's world is everyone's domain, we find ourselves in search of meaning through the spirit and the Light – two predominant images – used to bring us into realization, that this is what we are all in search of, or need. His allusions are to the salvation we must all seek to be in oneness with the creator God. As such the poems are trenchantly inspirational giving us hope, solace and empowerment to be at peace, whenever, or wherever we happen to be.

It's a primer for ALL of us, travellers on a bus, maxi, car, aeroplane or even the causeway of life. We can open the book at any point and find ready sustenance. The poet's voice is at times persuading, aiding, coaching one to take the hand of truth, be of good faith and follow the light in the true spirit of eternal belief, that all is possible, only commit to the belief that the triumphs is in finding the light that beckons.

This is a collection for all seasons.

Reynold Bassant M.A.
Post Graduate Dip. In HR,
Public Relations and Advertising.
Cultural Activist and Freelancing Writer.
Chairman, Naparima Bowl Board.

ACKNOWLEDGEMENTS

Thanks to my brother Mr. Willi Chen, Artist, Sculptor, Writer and Art Critic, for his insight into my poetic intuition and his encouragement throughout. Thanks also to Prof. Frank Birbalsingh, Fr. John Harricharan and Mr. Reynold Bassant for their critical reading of my poems and generous comments and Mrs. Vashtee Persad my Secretary of long standing for her computer skills and eye for translating my scribbles into legible print. Finally, thanks to my beloved wife Nazreen, whose sense of aesthetic design with word sounds and ideas, was a source of Inspiration in the creation of this volume.

CONTENTS

CREATION

In the Beginning
there was Nothing,
Neither space nor time
We were Nothing,
are Nothing
will be Nothing,
But for the Almighty Lord
the Creator,
whose Nature is to Be,
the First Cause,
the Uncaused Cause
of the Heavens
and the Earth,
the Land and the Sea,
Fishes deep in the Ocean,
Birds flapping skyward,
High Forests blooming yellow,
Animals a thousand species,
Till the coming of man,
to have Dominion
over all Creation.
Let us ponder
In a moment of stillness
The Immensity
of God's Power,
The Infinity of His Love.
Let us plead

with constancy
and resolve
to fulfill to perfection,
our measured portions
of duties and of work,
renewing others in their Trust,
gathering others in their Love,
before we finally return
to Eternity.
We need to buckle,
down on our knees,
cry out in repentance,
and bit by bit,
unshackle this burden of
the World
and its Gold
to find
a peace here,
And forever.

GOD IS WAITING

God is waiting
every moment, of every day,
He knows
we want to
and we can,
weakness keeps
dragging us down,
still He waits
and He waits,
with patience and
with Love.
Let us rise
and go now
and go and feel
His warm Embrace.

ONE IN LOVE

We were all made for Love,
from all Eternity
to all Eternity,
that all be One,
with the Father
through the Son
with the Holy Spirit,
Listening to the Divine
every moment of every day
rushing through traffic,
waiting on line,
or simply sipping coffee
on a wayside nook.

IN SILENCE

Seeing not with Our Eyes,
Hearing not with Our Ears,
Talking to God,
In an Intimacy of Love
Within.

TODAY NOW

We live Today
Now,
Not tomorrow,
that never comes,
Not yesterday
we left behind,
the little Good
we did
the Evil
to be undone,
and so much more.
We ponder
for a moment,
the Power of Repentance,
Lighting up our Spirit,
with an Irrepressible Joy
to Begin Again
Again and Again,
Today
Now.

TIME TO GO

It is time to go my friend,
It is time to go,
But where to my friend,
Where to?
The Hour is so late,
Where to?
The twilight darkens the Heavens,
The Lone Star in the Sky,
Darkness covers the Land, My Friend,
Where to
Where to?
To the Bright Light in the Distance,
the Home of Eternal Rest.
Let us go my friend,
let us go,
Before it is too late,
Too late, my friend,
Too late?
Never too late my friend
Never too late,
To a Home in the Distance,
A Home of Peace
and Rest.

BEGINNING AGAIN

Another chance,
another Grace,
absorbed in Silence,
motionless,
listening to the
Gentle Voice,
whispering within,
Repenting of Sins,
Remembering,
Repositioning
Strategies of Love,
and of Strength
Struggling constantly,
against Our Passions,
of Flesh and of Greed,
of Envy and our pompous
air of absurdity,
against Evil Forces,
ever prowling in clusters,
Day and Night.
Our strength is
in Repentance
Beckoning the Divine.
Do not be afraid.

THE LIGHT

We must not be filled
with Light,
But be
the Light,
spreading
to the end of the world,
Till the end of time.

WISDOM

It is Wisdom, profound,
to know that we know
But Little,
Greater still the Wisdom,
To know
where to gain such Wisdom.

THE CARTHUSIAN

Speaks in Silence

When you left
and vowed yourself
to Silence and Stability
to Chastity and Obedience
to Poverty
in your Little Cell,
Cold and Heavy with
Thick Walls, Silent,
Day and Night,
a Small Table
an over head light,
and you alone,
in Silence, listening
to God in Silence,
No word, Day
Nor Night,
a Constant Flow
of Rushing Waters,
from Heaven, on all sides,
of your Inner Being,
Filling you in an Ecstatic
Explosion of Joy,
and Meaning, and
Love for all those
you have left,

Friends, City folks,
Villagers under the Palm,
including those who
envied and despised you,
that all be gathered into
One Love Here
and Hereafter.
Your incessant cry,
from within,
travelling,
in repetitive waves,
on Wings of Infinity,
Unseen but felt
everywhere,
No where hidden,
from the Reaches of
The Absolute Being,
prompted by your
Love and Concern
your prayers,
Becoming more
and more,
Infinite in Power
and Reach.
We thank you
for reminding us,
to remain Rooted
in Place and Work,
Nailed, amidst
The Constant Crossfire,
of Shouts and
Screams of Pain, and

Malice, Man
becoming Beast,
Prowling the
streets Devouring
whoever —
where ever.
We must remain,
Faithful in
our Assignment,
Converting the Streets
and the Alleyways,
Into cells of Silence,
Contemplating the Rush,
of Madness,
Bringing one and all,
Every one,
Home.

ONLY A CREATURE

God created man,
Man did not
create God,
Man is only a steward,
Accountable till
 the End.

WITHOUT A CROSS

For York

I hope you are readying
for the next year of
long studies.
Nothing achieved,
without effort
without a cross
without an opportunity
to be made holy
in preparation for
God on Earth
God in heaven.
Keep up the struggle,
as I know you would,
spread the message
by example and
concern.
Obstacles appear
with regularity
the workings
of self love,
the lust of the eyes
the pull of the flesh
the boasts of power.

A SILENCE WITHIN

We discover ourselves
within Our Being
where dwelleth
the Source of all Being
our Pain and Anguish
Vanish
when We rest with Him,
in Silence
and in Peace.

FINDING GOD

We discover Science
through our head,
we find God
on our knees,
Knowing God
Is more
Than knowing Science.

IN THE BEGINNING

In the beginning
there was God.
Outside, there was nothing.
Neither you nor I
nor Darwin.
Nothing to evolve
neither dust
nor mist
no birds in the air
no fish in the sea
no crawling serpents
no lights no darkness
no day no night.
Only God,
always was
always is
always will
be everlasting.
Then God made the world,
    made everything
    the land and the sea
    the wind and
    the stars
the sun and the moon
filtering through palm leaves
softly on sand
down Mayaro.

IN CONTEMPLATION

Silence is the Voiceless
Prayer of the Soul,
the Word less
Language of love,
of God who IS,
The Eternal Presence,
The Eternal Silence,
of the Infinite Love
of Mercy
and of Power.
Seek out that Silence,
In your office ...... Silent,
Under the cool
Samaan spreading ...... Silent,
in the Factory,
Dead to the Constant
Drummings ...... Silent,
The Incessant Whistle,
of Conflict and of Stress ...... Silent.
Silence is the Language,
of the Stillness
of the Soul,
In the Intimacy,
of the Union of God,
The Father,
and God The Son,
And the Holy Spirit,

and You and Me,
Adopted Children,
In the Bosom of Love,
Inheritors of the Earthly,
and Heavenly Domains.

CALL TO HOLINESS

A Call to Holiness
is a Call for everyone,
To seek such Holiness,
is to seek a Silence,
Listening to a Voice
Within,
In Silence,
Away from the Hum
of Traffic,
Motoring Beetles flashing Fast,
No Screams, No blasts,
Going Home
In Silence.

IN CONTENTMENT

Teach us to be content O Lord,
what ever befalls us
Good or Evil,
nothing is stable
everything is moving.
Hopefully
To a Blessed End.

SEEING THE LIGHT

God became Man
that man may
Become God,
what a confusion
of mind
and of Purpose.
A Light in the Distance
is Calling us Home.

DR. WILFRED ALBUQUERQUE

Ever since Ruth sent news
of sadness caused by
sinister cells, rude and
unruly, advancing, unchecked
by all of man's mighty
science and powers,
I have been remembering
    you in prayer
    at Daily Mass,
the unbloody continuation
of Our Lord's total giving
of His Sacrificial Blood
and Flesh, torn apart,
hanging limp on the Cross,
for my wickedness and sins,
and yours too,
and those of the whole world,
of every single living
    being,
under every bush,
in every city corner,
for this is the ultimate prayer,
the Infinite Prayer of souls,
barely whispering, at the back of the chapel,
    barely lit,
in this speck of an island,
in this speck of a planet,

in this vast universe,
stretching,
further and further,
into unfathomable
Limitless
Nothingness.

Writing you
is like writing myself.
We both are nearing the end,
after three score and
more years,
walking along the winding
roads, in Winter Galway,
bicycle lights flashing
on wet roads,
hustling in the early morn
darkness to Aula Maxima,
to Physics and Dissection,
under the Library, for
Experimental Medicine,
with Prof. Lavelle.
Such an excitement
of improvising Jacob's
metal tins into
cheap and cosy
C57BL mice cages,
with small black eyes
darting everywhere.

You struggled,
Bill Choo Foo, the mountain

Heavy weight, Basketball
Bull struggled,
we all struggled,
and escaped Prof. O'Donnell's
silent stares,
Prof. Kennedy's word economy.
Later you shepherded
the sick and elderly across
the Channel
and saw them washed
in the Waters of Lourdes,
and healed,
the Lame walk
the Blind see,
where there was
Faith and absolute
Trust in the Power
of Jesus,
Not as in Nazareth,
where there was not
even a miracle,
as His fellow villagers doubted,
were even vexed,
'Is he not the Carpenter's Son?'

WHO IS GOD

I am
Who am,
Eternally Present,
No Past
No Future,
Eternally Present,
Entering time's History
In Bethlehem,
a Baby
noiseless,
cold in straw,
Defenceless,
unable to speak
to ask,
Dependent on man
Totally,
learning to walk,
stumbling,
learning to talk,
the idioms
echoing
of Jewish customs,
playing amongst
the wooden shavings,
washed cleaned for supper,
What ordinariness,
In Time

In Deeds,
Finding your
Majestic Infinity
in the Simplicity
of your Humanity
and Your Oneness
with us, that
we may approach
You,
Find You
and Love you,
for your Unbelievable
Incomprehensible
Love for us, men.

RACING THROUGH LIFE

Running through life
at a fast pace,
on the right lane
not crossing over,
not delaying
nor distracted,
by dazzling trinkets,
Calves of Gold,
Concrete towers gleaming,
in the morning sun,
Night life pleasures
Neon lights flashing,
Dulling the senses
Depressing the Spirit.
Keep on running,
Hear His call
He is waiting,
Keep on running.
Evil forces in clusters,
every where,
even in your mind,
in your senses.
Keep on listening
to His Voice,
Confident of your prize.

PUFFS OF AIR

What is anything
But everything,
Puffs of air,
Power or Pleasure,
Blustering dust in the wind.
Let the Infinite
Infuse in you
an inner peace,
a stillness and
    a silence
of Ethereal Bliss,
    Eternally.

LOVE

Life is about Loving.
Without Love
Is an emptiness
on earth
A beginning of Hell.

Love is a pair of
little cravats,
yellow, twittering
on the lawn grass.

Seeking, you will find
True love
in everything
in everyone
on Earth.
Then a love
so rapturous
ever expanding
ever filling
for all Eternity.

FAREWELL O' HENRY

Inching closer
to the End,
Grey hairs falling,
Bald,
Shuffling,
in mind and in gait,
past midnight,
still awake,
in contemplating
restlessness.
Who are we,
where from
whither we go?
Farewell O' Henry,
your Legacy of the Ordinary,
worked over and over again,
to Perfection
in Design and Details,
maturing in Faith
and Holiness
Every day,
responding to an early call,
like those in Galilee,
chosen before time,
to make Holy your
Work and your Life,
In total self giving.
Farewell O' Henry.

GOD'S COMING

What manner of Coming
is yours O Lord,
Creator of the Mountains
Valleys and Dreams,
Born Helpless,
in a cave in a Distant Country
without family nor friends,
warmed only by an Ox,
Chewing cud,
a Faithful Donkey,
standing in docile readiness,
Bracing against wet winds,
Whistling cold
through cracks,
in the cavernous spaces,
lifting high the
Bedding of Straw,
Leaving little Jesus,
Shivering, all alone,
in the cold.

IN GOD

Being immersed
in God
who made the World,
not in the world
made by God.

IN RECOLLECTION

Regrouping old friends
and families
from the past,
walking barefooted
    to school,
under the Tamarind tree.
How many have left
we don't know
    nor care.
We need to listen to
    an inner voice,
sounding louder and louder
with every day,
longer and longer
with every moment,
passed in Stillness
and in Silence.

Away from the booming
And the booming,
we need to pause for a moment,
In silence,
away from the City
Walls crumbling on sand,
burying souls
in despair and forever.
Haven't we too,

been stifling our passions
　of love
and of mercy?
Are we not guilty
　of indifference
in finding the lost sheep
identifying the Saviour
to the many
　so many
wandering, aimlessly
without a Shepherd?

OBSTINACY

The Obstacle to Love,
in this Journey
of Joys,
and of Sorrows,
is our Stubbornness
in Sin.
Only the Fire
of Repentance,
can Scorch out
the Evil,
Ever Crawling within,
overflowing us,
with a Brimful of Love.

CHINA DOCTORS RETURNING HOME

Some thoughts
on the Life of Jesus,
from the enclosed pages
will light up the pathways
of your life,
sublimate your
work so technical,
so arduous and professional.
I leave you
the New Testament,
which details the Life of Christ
on earth two thousand years
ago,
whose mission was and is
to redeem all men from sin
and punishment, you,
your wife, your child,
your parents and families,
your colleagues, your
patients and their families,
the government officials
and their friends and
families, rich and poor
educated and uneducated,
those in Beijing in
Tiensin, in Xian,
in India, America and

Trinidad and Tobago
Everyone, from every corner of
the world,
without exception,
by working hard,
with your same dedication
and competence, now
for the Love of Christ and
the love for people, love of country.
In this way we grow
little by little in
inner joy and peace,
and develop ourselves
and others
and making
them rich and happy
here and here after.

IMMENSITY OF GOD'S LOVE

The Immensity of God's
Goodness, rests in us
Hidden in Silence
Bringing a Comfort
of Peace and Serenity,
a Security Absolute
against all fears of
Evil or Mishaps,
for us and our
Family and Friends,
and all People
around and afar.
His Coming,
the Sacrificial Cleansing
of Sins, all Sins
accumulated down the ages
and those yet to come
till the end of time,
Finally expurgated
by His Atonement
On The Cross, His Broken
Body hanging limp,
bleeding, not for a
minute or two,
gasping and gasping
in slow death
for hours.

Let us Kneel
in Silent Repentance,
for our Sins,
Daring to invite
Him to
fill Our Being,
with His Sacred Presence,
Together with Our Father
and Our Holy Spirit,
to Dwell within us
in an intimacy of
Friendship,
so longed for, since,
the beginning
of Time,
The incomprehensive
Love of the Eternal Father,
For simple creatures,
of Nothingness
like You and Me.

THE YOUTH OF TIME

Outside the Soul,
Time revolves
Metrically around the Sun.
Within the Soul,
is a Meeting Place,
of Time
with Infinity,
It stays its age,
Youthful immutability
A foretaste of Peace,
and Heavenly Dimensions.

OUR GOAL

When we fix our purpose
In the distance,
what was important
becomes trivial,
what was trivial
becomes important.

APRIL RAIN

Rain keeps dripping from a
melancholy sky,
keeps falling through
   silent leaves,
cars splashing through
wet streets,
men crouching home,

Contemplating God
An Ocean of Goodness
filling every crevice
of our being flooding us into a
Transcending Greatness,
God-like in Presence
   and Power,
inspiring us into action,
accomplishing Deeds
of Love and Mercy,
of Super Human Strength
sacrifice and dimension,

If only we can surrender
our stubborn resistance
to the gentle whisperings of
   the Holy Spirit,
if only we can crush

our Self Sufficient Egos
and our Self-willed
    Arrogance,
if only we let the Grace
from Heaven filter
slowly into our Souls
like Raindrops falling
from the sky.

RECONNECTING WITH BRIAN

It is a joy
Sean found you
in the Galway fields,
    A treasure that was polished
    A heart that was sealed
at Merlin Park
by Dr. Kneafsey and the gentle
doctor from Kerala
where many a soul
has bloomed in Holiness
like St Alphonsa
like St Xavier
who raised twenty people
    from the dead
whose body remains uncorrupt
in The Goa Cathedral.
In these days in Ireland,
Amongst the ISIS and
    the Bokas
there is a fierceness
of battle unheard of
in the history of the world,
    A dismemberment
    A beheading.
In the heart of some
A cauldron of fiery hate
    Is brewing

A stirring by spirits
of Evil
from which
we ought to pray
For delivery
constantly
and continuously.

BEING FIRST

The First shall be
The Last,
The Last shall
Be First,
Being first is always
a risk.
Whatever our place,
First or Last,
or Somewhere
in between,
Unknown,
Unseen,
Unsung,
Staying Our Place,
Steadying our Self,
moving constantly,
Upwards,
Inspite our failings,
moving constantly
Upwards
always with Help
from Above,
Is Being First
Without a Risk
Before Eternity.

HOPE

Can our Society be saved?
The Nations of the World
be saved?
Can we be saved,
you and I?
We know not yet.
We need the Gift of Fear,
the Gift of Vigilance,
Faith and Hope.
We need to Pray,
and keep on Praying,
with Words
And with Deeds,
Always,
Only then
we will not be afraid.

SEEDS OF LOVE

Seeding Christ,
Into the Hearts of Men,
Copting the Holy Spirit,
Fanning the Flames,
Deep within,
Blazing Fires of Love.

THE WORD OF GOD

It is good
to read the word of man.
It is better
to read the word of God.
Before God
Man is nothing.

TO PROF. FRANCIS KELLY

President of Catholic Association
of Scientist and Engineers USA

You were so kind to send
Your lovely photos regaled like
a Knight of Jesus and your
marriage back in 1964. What a
handsome couple chosen in
Heaven to fulfill a divine vocation
to people the earth with
   good children and
10 grandchildren counting, and to
sanctify your professional
work as an International
Scientist and to begin again,
after a brief sadness
sending off your beloved
companion of so many years
to a place of continuous
and expanding happiness.
The Holy Spirit is at you again.
The Scientists and the Engineers
the Professionals need you more
to fill their souls with the Food
   from Heaven.
   What hunger
   What darkness
   What violence
In the world today!

CRUMPLED IN AGE

Crumpled with age
crooked on stick,
swaggering in mind,
still stamping
in anger.
What a waste, never too late
for Repentance,
Time for Peace.

TIT BITS

Let us not belittle
the little things of love,
Reminding of the Presence
the Infinite Being of Love,
Hovering over us,
solicitous of every hair,
every computer click,
every Face Book twitter,
Driving through long lanes of traffic,
Tired, heading home.

CRYSTAL SOUL

The soul is a crystal
lighted up in the Sun
Sin is a blanket
covering it
in Darkness

BECOMING LOVE

To live is to Die,
To the World
To the Flesh
To One's Will.

To live is to Die,
Of Love,
Becoming Love,
One in Love,
With the Divine.

DOKTOR MAE WAN HO

I am new,
to your Prolific
outflow of Living Science.
Your mind so fertile and scintillating,
like a Star from the East
bearing gifts to
the Child of the Common Good,
the rich and the poor
the blind and the lame,
your Light, Celestial
like a Rainbow
sparkling spots of red and gold
dancing to a quantum rhythm.
You see the Work of the Infinite
Heisenberg waves,
shimmering through space
through millions and millions
of breathless miles,
Incomprehensible
Overwhelming
Ordered
to every millisec,
not by chance,
But by Design
before Time began
Becoming
Becoming
from Here
to Eternity.

POESY

Poetry is an outflow
of Emotion, in words
and in thought,
Resonating in the hearts of
men, Healing
and Enlightening,
in rhythm and in music,
like Rich Port
swaying in Dance,
Cane Arrows
Fluffy in the Fields.

VANITY

What can Man know,
what can he do,
so limited his strength
so miniscule his mind,
Such Pompous Nonsense,
Before the Vastness
of the Divine,
Cosmic in Dimension.
We need a silence
to contemplate
the Divine,
pleading for more,
and more,
from the fullness
of Life
Eternal.

THE MORAL LAWS

Physical Laws
are the Laws
of the Body,
Moral Laws
are Laws
of the Soul.
We can manipulate
the Laws of Nature
not change them.
We can pick and choose
the Moral Laws,
to the detriment
of Our Being.
Perfect fulfillment
of the Moral Laws
is The Way
The Only Way
To Perfection.

THE SPIRIT OF GOD

Listening to the Spirit of God
not the Spirit of Man,
listening to Our Angel
soothing our Soul
with Peace.

THE PRESIDENT VISITS
NORTH HALL 2016

For His Excellency
President Anthony Carmona

Though days have passed,
nay weeks since your
Presidential Coming,
If we have forgotten,
not the little ones in brown,
their little hands,
raised in rank chorus,
singing songs of love
in enchanting innocence,
so wanting in us
ensnared in intrigue and
grabbing viciousness.
So much evil prowling,
so many bodies sprawling on the streets.
Your visit was refreshing,
leaving the stiff salute
and High Honours
on the door steps,
embracing us with
a warm earthliness.
In the silent stillness

of the softly lit Oratory,
you were subsumed

by the Divine Presence,
of the Consecrated Bread
of Sacred Substance.
You emerged enveloped,
by a Mystical experience,
unable to control,
a spontaneous outflow
of a joyous message,
bold and urgent,
to launch out,
into the streets
into the shacks every where,
in Kingston, in Mandeville, in Montego Bay,
bringing memories of Mona,
a tinge of sadness and of joy,
of a wonderful friend,
lost in St. Lucia.
You remembered
to tap and kept tapping,
the shoulder of a genius,
in your words,
Willi Chen, writer, sculptor,
creator of the effervescent gem,

the emerald blue sparkle,
Eyeing us
at every turn,
unveiled by you
for us and all posterity.

NO FEAR

Why are we afraid
when God is with us,
He is the Power,
extending beyond
   Time
   And Space.

LOVING THE WORLD

We must not be
Buried in our Riches,
Blind to the needs
of the man on the wayside,
Rummaging through Rubbish,
Crumpled in the Cold.
We must love
the World with a Passion,
the World is Good,
made by God.
We must not turn
it to Evil,
for ourselves only,
for our Family
for our Country,
Neglecting our neighbours
Nor those in Faraway places.

WRAPPED IN GOD

Walking in Silence
amongst the Trees,
Footsteps falling on the leaves,
a Gift of Love
unmerited,
not listening
even to the
Black and Yellow Semp,
twittering amongst
the Sikiyea leaves
sitting under the Bamboo
arches,
a Cathedral of
Heavenly Presence.

IN RETREAT

What a Grace, Chosen
to be away
from the rush,
Here on these Hills,
Looking over the Cocoa,
The Yellow Poui Flowing,
Down to the Plains,
in Silence,
except for Nature's Sounds,
Wind whistling through Leaves,
Kiskidees Kingly Perched,
in Trumpeting Chorus,
Rhapsodic Refrains,
in Non-Stop Encores,
in Silence,
like Trappist Monks,
in Hooded File
Past Midnight,
Listening to the
Voice of ABBA,
Repeating and Repeating,
softly within,
One with God,
God with us,
In an Intimacy of
a Father and a Son,

a Friend and his Family,
the Spirit Flowing Fast,
Ever Widening,
All Becoming One,
One Becoming All.

BISHOP JAVIER ECHEVARRÍA'S
VISIT TO TRINIDAD

Just a mite of a Gift
in gratitude of your coming,
a foretaste of The Coming,
at the end of time,
in memory of your
unique Triune intimacy
of lived closeness with
two canonized Saints,
Beloved Saint Josemaria
Escriva, Founder of
The Work of God,
and Blessed Bishop Portillo,
Successor, most faithful
follower in his footsteps,
and mirror of the Earthly
Saintliness of St. Josemaria
Escriva.

In gratitude of your visit
to this island,
dedicated to the Triune God

God the Father
God the Son
And the Holy Spirit

one and only
One God,
by the brave and holy Explorer,
Franciscan Tertiary Christopher Columbus,
much maligned by enemies of the church.
    Praying constantly
    with increasing trust,
    awaiting the fruits
    of the Holy Spirit
    the children of
    our Father's love.

LANTANA CONFERENCE CENTRE

Lantana Conference Centre
and Hospitality School

rests on a small hill
in Gran Couva,
overlooking cocoa and yellow poui
far from the city's jamming
and noise
where we can listen to
God speaking through the
corn birds and lush trees
spreading down the valley,
contemplating
the unease
and dissatisfaction of
ourselves, our home and our work
our country and our world.

Where we can discover the
corruption reaching the
inner recesses of our being,
where we can think clearly
with the Divine in the Divine
and plan a path of justice and peace
for others
and ourselves.
Where we can discover

and be surprised by
the abundance of gifts
given by God,
partly buried,
to be unleashed,
bit by bit, in a journey
to perfection and fullness
of love for all people,
young and old
rich, poor and lame.
literate and illiterate
of all colourful shades,
every where, in the refineries
in hospitals, the police stations,
the bus stands, business centres and
in parliament.
In the sea,
in the sky
that all may begin
that journey
with Peace
and Optimism to
Timeless Happiness.
We can also be tempted
by another path,
of Greed Power and Lusts,
of Hate. A stabbing and
a stabbing,
an overpowering
madness of sensuality,
breeding Dens of Evil,
intrigue and selfishness,

slipping down the road
of stubborn pomposity pain
and torture,
ending in an agony,
fixed in suffering
Eternally.

Lantana Conference Centre
and Hospitality School
will provide the opportunity
of workshops
retreats, seminars,
training people to
seek perfection where ever
at work
at home
in the fields of play,
doing things well,
with honesty and competence,
with promptness and perseverance,
with sacrifice
and humility
as a service of love.

We invite you
to be part of this
adventure, to give some
time, your experience
or your skills to dream
Dreams
which with the help of God
will always fall short.

A MOMENT OF SILENCE

Where ever we are,
whatever the moment,
it's never too late
to take a pause,
on the stairway
on the street
in the air,
by the Bus stop
by the Stop Light,
High in the office.
to reflect for a second,
whither we have come
whither we go,
to withdraw in silence
into our Soul,
settling the Voice of peace
straightening our path,
in ever deepening
Repentance.

COME O' HOLY SPIRIT

O Holy Spirit
How can You
fit into my Soul
so tiny a speck
in the Cosmic Infinitude,
so willing to enkindle
a blaze of Love
for all peoples,
not only families and friends,
even enemies,
so willing to search out
the far reaches for
Every Soul, we have
forgotten and lost
in whatever Corner
whatever City
or Country
for friends misplaced
by our careless
and obsessive self.
We trust in your
Power to search
every Corner,
No Room
No Hotel
Under no Bridge,
can hide any soul
recoverable for
Eternity.

SIGHTING CHRIST THIS CHRISTMAS

Jesus touched the eyes
of the two blind men,
and their faith
made them see.

Many do not see
Christ in Christmas.
They are physically blind
or spiritually so.

Sin covers them
with a darkness,
they becoming blind
in their blindness.

They ought to shout to Jesus
who is passing by
and shout more and more
above the dissuading crowds
distracting
that they may see.

Only true repentance
through confession
can cleanse them
of their lusting and their greed.

Only then
through the Power of Christ
The Baby in the Crib
becomes a blazing light
of a million stars
this Christmas.

A NEW YEAR

Every year
a new Beginning
every day
a new resolution.
When will we stop dreaming!
Time moves so fast.
We need to begin
again and again,
Now, every moment of
every day,
and Put into Practice
the little plans,
yielding in the end
a Handful,
Rich in Harvest.

THE CHEN CLAN HOME COMING 2017

Bringing Happiness
is your Home Coming,
Flapping down like Egrets,
from Northern Wilderness,
spreading into Family
Nooks, purified of
Refinery fumes by a
coziness of Ancestral
Lineage of Love,
Asaw, Ashook,
Shook May, Agoon
Apo and more,
sounds all fading
into corruption
by Tongue and TV.

WHO IS SHE

Who is She
that Blackeyed Beauty
smooth face, hair swept back,
That barefooted girl
from California.
Her Soong style top, mottled blue,
buttoned to the neck,
Her eyes a freshness of love,
for family, friends and enemies,
a love gushing forth,
from a heart constantly cleansed,
and re-cleansed by
a constant flow of
Gratuitous Living Waters.
Who has pinned a thousand dishes,
Bringing Home Flavours
of Far away Places,
blending Cultures in
a Callaloo of Fragrances,
Fine tuning
Time and Temperature,
to a Holiness of Perfection,
Every roast, crispy brown,
Oak smoked, See Yow tanned.
what Ethereal tastes,
Lifting Spirits to the Sky.
Who is She!

BELOVED

What a joy
to be united
before we were born,
long before Sandford St,
in the mind of Our Lord,
manifesting His love
in us that together,
one in one
more and more
moment by moment
sharing his Heavenly Blessings,
His Divine Joy
in an ecstatic union
in ethereal happiness.

OLD FRIENDS

Your prompt response
is a joy of old friends met.
Thanks to Dong and Rebecca,
stalwarts of efficient loyalty
who deserve a shot of Mao Tai
if you were here
in the sunshine and sands
below Palms swaying in the steady breeze
in Maracas or Mayaro.
Let us hope your positive action
is reflection of the science
beneath the slides.

CONTEMPLATING GOLF

Let the Divine
   light up the pathways
   of Life.
Empowering the Spirit
   with unbelievable strength
   fostering a stillness
   of inner peace,
Steadying the mind
   the swings
   the chips
   and the putt
In the mounting tension
   of a million faces
   waiting
   and waiting
   in breathless silence.

LIFE IS LOVE

Rejection of one's life
is the rejection of Love,
to be without Love,
is to be empty,
Sad and Lonely

BEING IN GOD

We have the Lord,
the Joy
of the World,
who made all things,
who knows all things,
can do all things,
Why be sad
Or lonely!

EMERITUS PROFESSOR

For Frank

So good to know
your mind is firing
past your years.
What Emeritus
for folks like you!
What is stroke
for a Georgetown beoy!
They never hear bout
Cricket
The fresh breeze
in the Blood
divinised
by the Spirit
Holy and sublime.
Still time for learning
    time to reflect
    for an inner peace
    in this endless
    struggle
    against pain and conflict.
May you be immersed
in the peace
of the Almighty
Here on earth
And Eternity.

80 AND STILL GOING

Giving thanks going past 80,
much yet to finish
not many years left,
measuring work
in limited portions,
shuffling from shelf to shelf,
no idleness in you
squeezed through fingers
toughened with work,
your voice still clear
like a school boy,
your hearing as sharp,
your Spirit a sparkle
youthful and clean.
How you long
to hear the children
you taught
sing hymns of Jesus
shaking the floor boards
at Esperanza C.M.
or causing raukus
care-free under the Samaan Tree.

Where are they now
where have they gone,
the little you have done
and have repented for all
you did not do,
or did so badly.

FAREWELL TO NIALL

Thank you Gerard
for your sense of communion,
sending a sad note
of O'Donohoe's leave
for a far away place,
more familiar to the older folks,
muffed in black wrap,
silently muttering to Heaven.
Gone are those generations
who sacrificed so many,
handsome, young and smiling,
To light up the darkness
In the East, in the West,
In India, and Africa
even the Caribbean.

IN GRATITUDE

To Gerard

You are a savior almost like Our Lord,
curing ten men, leprous,
sores, crawling in their faces
and only one returned,
his face kissing
the feet of our Lord,
he shouting in Joyful Gratitude.
Were there not ten?
Where are the others?
Get up and go away.
Your faith has saved you.

I can't thank you enough,
your exemplary promptness
confounding the Noon Day
Devil of procrastination,
careless work and laziness
in our feeble attempts
serving the people
    all people
for the Glory of God.

THE CROSS

Never a need,
to look for the Cross,
It meets us everyday,
every hour
of every day,
a Harsh word,
a Spit on the Face,
a Highway puncture,
or Just missing the Bus,
The Will of God
or The Will of Man,
or Just the rawness
of the circumstance,
whatever,
whenever,
Let us
carry the Cross,
Bearing it Silently,

Becoming the Cross, slowly
Bit by Bit.
A Living Cross,
Breathing it slowly,
Breathing out calmly,
with a patience,
an inner Peace
and an inner Silence.

PRAYER

If we do not sow
we do not reap.
If we do not ask
we do not receive
we must intensify
our prayers
persevere in our asking
daring in our demands
persisting like little
children
enwrapping the Father of
Love with Love.

DATA DIGESTION

True knowledge,
Stone Dead in Books
In Electronic Spaces,
must come alive,
Assimilated in our minds,
Circulating in our Cells
Imprinted in our Genes
Refashioned
Recalibrated
Resurrected,
In a Free Personal Apparition,
The Fruit of Reflection,
the Touch of Creative Flair
in Every One
imaged in the Likeness,
of the Creator
Genius Almighty.

RELATIVITY OF SINS

There are some,
sharp brained and gifted,
who see Good,
calling it Evil
who see Evil,
calling it good,
Descendants of our
First Ancestors,
who sought to be
Architects of their lives,
Determining Good
and Evil,
Becoming Gods
unto themselves,
Evil nestling
In their malice.
Sins becoming non-Sins,
Non-sins becoming Sins,
a Darkness of confusion
a Nothingness of Confession.

STUBBORNNESS

Do not be afraid,
the Arms of God,
so loving in Mercy,
are Towering Cranes,
Tenderly Powered by
a child-like simplicity,
Lifting stubbornness in sin,
like boulders,
in our pathway
to Heaven.

THE BEGINNING OF LIFE

In Our beginning
We were
Two half cells, uniting
In spousal love,
Birthing a single Cellular Being,
Full of Life and Potency,
Scarred by
The continuous corruption
of our Genes and Mind
by Adam's Original Curse,
compounded year after year
by our sins of Flesh and Spite,
Greed Envy and Arrogance,
Enshrouding us in Evil,
by a Dark Stubbornness.
Let us listen
in the Silence of our Soul
for that persistent
Alien Voice of Conscience
Commanding and Authoritative,
searing off
the layers
of sins and of selfishness,

we becoming more,
and more,
Immersed in God.

MATURING IN HOLINESS

Growing in Holiness,
Every moment
of every day
Is the Will of the Father,
Dwelling deep within,
And the Will of the Lord
who saved us
Hanging on His Wrists,
His weight pushing
into Nails through His Feet
and the Will of the Holy Spirit,
scattering Evil Spirits
streaking through the sky,
into Dungeons of Darkness,
where there is continuous
fighting, gnashing and grinding
of teeth, no eating, no sleeping
chained in pain forever.

GOLFING AT DORAL

For Grayson

Your tips made me a Tiger
without the stripes
the distance.
I like the image
Michelle Wie's right
Angle
hands low like a
master
back spinning the
chips.
Man today is tormented
by incessant Noise
and Rush,
Man needs to pause
and Breathe in Silence
Alone with God.
Inner Solitude
in Silence
is a Gift from God
granted through
The Goodness of God
On knees of
Repentance
to Souls
cleansed of Sins.

FEARS OF CHILDHOOD

Walking jigger footed
Through the Coconuts,
Facing snorting Monsters,
Horned Black Bisons,
Of Nether world Scariness,
Facing the lipayed hut dweller,
Grey beard tapering
To his belly, dhoti wrapped,
With wooden beads slithering
Around his neck, wrinkled
His face dotted,
Red and White
A Frightening mirage,
Keeper of the Underworld.

LOVE - UNSELFISH

Our Absolute Happiness
depends on our Absolute giving,
the measure we give
is the measure we receive.
The Joy of Peace
Beginning here
Extends into Eternity.
What an Expanding
Happiness!

IN FLOW OF GRACES

Opening the Channels
of our Being
to a continuous inflow
of Graces,
Filling our Souls
to the brim,
Stamping the signs of
the Cross,
on our Shoulders
and our Chest
and on our Torso,
Lancing a wound
at Our Side,
Gushing a flow
of Love,
with Fruits,
perfumed and luscious,
Nourishing many,
near and far,
Instilling a Peace
Of soul
Lighting up all
with a glow of Joy.

KEEP GOING FRANCIS

I often wondered about you
and the Catholic Association of Scientists
so needed in these times
of smoothness
and treachery
like some
Supreme Injustices.

What fiery sadness,
what pain,
here and
here after,
for many,
Whether they believe
or believe not,
if they don't kneel
In Repentance.

SPARKLING AGAIN

When we lose
that spring in our steps,
that sparkle in our voice,
that smile from a heart
Full of love,
It's a sign of self love,
Even of Sin
or Evil passing by,
We need to kneel,
in Spirit if not in Body,
and ask for forgiveness,
Increasing Our Trust.
A Baby in the Arms
of Our Mother.

JOY

Move with Joy
filled with Joy
we are the
Joy of the Lord
why be sad
or lonely .
We have the Lord
who knows all things,
can do all things
Creator of all things
You and I
and always
Forgiving.

EAST MEETS WEST

For Dennis

It was great, Madrid CNAPS VII,
overlooking Real Madrid
field of Gold manicured.
Wine, Good friends and laughter,
what more !
Thank God
and thank you Damian and others.
I would have liked to
learn of your Cambridge
and Oxford experiences.
A real East meets West.

Scientists are we
Men and Women,
all gifted from Heaven
with Time Senses and
Mobility,
with an intuitive gift
of understanding the
hand work of the Creator,
the Laws Eternal,
Linking Genes, Molecules
and Electrons, in a
Dynamic order of
Fluidity and Perfection,

Man moving smoothly
manipulating matter
into Machines, Robots
and Rockets, Criss Crossing
The Cosmos,
with instant speed,
But where to
all this frenetic frenzy
Where to!
Now that our joints grating,
Hands in Tremor
Our mind foggy
our speech dribbling incoherent,
Where to
Where to my friends!

IMMERSED IN PRAYER

We must be
immersed in Prayer
everywhere
day and night
night and day
continuously and
constantly
eating drinking working
with families
with friends
under the palms
sipping coconut
scanning the horizon.

SILENCE

Seeking God in Silence,
seeing Him in Silence,
listening to Him,
embracing Him in Silence
the beginning of Eternity
of Silence
and in Silence.
Silence is the word of God,
the Solitude of Eternity,
All becoming One
One Becoming All,
in an Absolute
Eternity
of Expanding Silence.

SPACE IN TIME

Space and Time
  Co Exist.
Where there is Space
There is Time.
Where there is Time
There is Space.
Without Space
There is no Time.
Space is the
Measure of Time.
Where there is neither
Space nor Time
There is Infinity.
The Infinity of God
  WHO IS.
The Infinity of Heaven
The Infinity of Happiness
In the Infinity of God.

OUR HOME IN THE SNOW

For Frank

The New Year
in your New Home,
almost buried in Snow,
Coldest Winter,
Country for Bears
And Eskimos.
We from Berbice,
And from Basta Hall
can't stop shivering,
with nose Bleeding
Toes numbed to the Bones.
Not within the cosiness
of you and Norma.
A glass of wine or Vintage
Demerara
will lift any Spirit
high so high.
And making Holy the Cold
and the Pain
the softly falling snow,
elevating the Spirit
even more

in a harmony of Union
with the Spirit of the Lord
a mystery of Love
of Mystical Dimension.

ALL IN ONE

We are the branches
Christ is the Vine,
Christ lives in our neighbour
as Christ lives in us,
His Blood courses
through our veins.
If we repent of our ways of sin
our greed and our fleshly lusts
exploiting others
or exploited by them,
with our virtues and our faults
we became One in All,
All in One with,
the Heavenly Father,
the Son and the Holy Spirit.

LIFE'S TIME LIMIT

We should live
every day
like one condemned.
Our time fixed
before Eternity,
Death trembling us
with fear.
Our nonchalant and careless
ways we need
to rectify,
ascending bit by bit,
to that Hill
of Prayer and Pain
where Repentance
can snap the chains
of our wild sensuality
of Greed and Hate,
cauterizing the inner corruption
of the selfishness in our Being.

Freed by the merciful
Father of Love

MYSTERY OF MAN

The Body in the Soul
The Soul in the Body
in a mystery
of Intimacy
A secrecy of Being
what a marvelous Union,
A Union of Body
in the Soul
Of Soul in the Body
of Matter in the Spirit
of Spirit in the Matter.
What a mystery
an inexplicable
mystery of Man
who is.

WHAT POWER, O DEATH

Will we be afraid
when the Hour Comes!
Will there be time
to repent
for our misdeeds,
   In our words
   In our thoughts
   In our omissions
of doing good
of forgiving
   bringing the peace of God
   the Joy and the Happiness
   settling slowly
   into Our Hearts
   and into Our Souls!

THE LAST FOUR THINGS

In our Journey
through life,
through its pain
and its suffering
we need to ponder
on the Four Last Things,
over and over
again and again
Death Judgment
Hell and Heaven.
We are so Addicted,
Blinded by the Power and the Riches,
and the Lusts of the Flesh,
We tend to suppress
The Eternal Truths of Life.
They should stand out
on our Dashboards,
in our Hospital beds,
or in our Office.
We are not Manic,
nor Depressive,
we are not Academic,
nor Nobel Scientists,
we are just simply
Philosophers Ordinaire,
knowing where we are,
reminding where

we are going,
always Scanning our steps,
Rectifying our misses,
to enter Eternity,
without any Baggage
without any Blemish,
nor Fear,
only with
the Smile
of a little Child.

DIVINE LIFE

It is the Will of
The Father,
that we become
like Him,
Eating His Flesh
Drinking His Blood,
Sharing His Life,
an Incomprehensible Gift
of Love,
of the Creator
of Everything
Seen and Unseen.

Printed in the United States
By Bookmasters